# ROALD DAHL'S

# THE BFG

# MAD LIBS®

D1361579

by Leigh Olsen

**PSS!**
PRICE STERN SLOAN
An Imprint of Penguin Random House

PRICE STERN SLOAN
Penguin Young Readers Group
An Imprint of Penguin Random House LLC

Mad Libs format copyright © 2016 by Price Stern Sloan,
an imprint of Penguin Random House LLC. All rights reserved.

Text copyright © 2016 by Roald Dahl Nominee Ltd. All rights reserved.

Concept created by Roger Price & Leonard Stern

Published by Price Stern Sloan,
an imprint of Penguin Random House LLC,
345 Hudson Street, New York, New York 10014.
Printed in the USA.

ISBN 978-0-399-53948-0
1 3 5 7 9 10 8 6 4 2

# MAD LIBS

# INSTRUCTIONS

MAD LIBS® is a game for people who don't like games!
It can be played by one, two, three, four, or forty.

## ● RIDICULOUSLY SIMPLE DIRECTIONS

In this tablet you will find stories containing blank spaces where words
are left out. One player, the READER, selects one of these stories. The
READER does not tell anyone what the story is about. Instead, he/she asks
the other players, the WRITERS, to give him/her words. These words are
used to fill in the blank spaces in the story.

## ● TO PLAY

The READER asks each WRITER in turn to call out a word—an adjective or
a noun or whatever the space calls for—and uses them to fill in the blank
spaces in the story. The result is a MAD LIBS® game.

When the READER then reads the completed MAD LIBS® game to the other
players, they will discover that they have written a story that is fantastic,
screamingly funny, shocking, silly, crazy, or just plain dumb—depending
upon which words each WRITER called out.

## ● EXAMPLE (*Before* and *After*)

"_____ !" he said _____
             EXCLAMATION                                    ADVERB

as he jumped into his convertible _____ and
                                              NOUN

drove off with his _____ wife.
                         ADJECTIVE

"_____ OUCH _____ !" he said _____ STUPIDLY _____
             EXCLAMATION                                    ADVERB

as he jumped into his convertible _____ CAT _____ and
                                              NOUN

drove off with his _____ BRAVE _____ wife.
                         ADJECTIVE

# MAD LIBS

# QUICK REVIEW

In case you have forgotten what adjectives, adverbs, nouns, and verbs are, here is a quick review:

An ADJECTIVE describes something or somebody. *Lumpy*, *soft*, *ugly*, *messy*, and *short* are adjectives.

An ADVERB tells how something is done. It modifies a verb and usually ends in "ly." *Modestly*, *stupidly*, *greedily*, and *carefully* are adverbs.

A NOUN is the name of a person, place, or thing. *Sidewalk*, *umbrella*, *bridle*, *bathtub*, and *nose* are nouns.

A VERB is an action word. *Run*, *pitch*, *jump*, and *swim* are verbs. Put the verbs in past tense if the directions say PAST TENSE. *Ran*, *pitched*, *jumped*, and *swam* are verbs in the past tense.

When we ask for A PLACE, we mean any sort of place: a country or city (*Spain*, *Cleveland*) or a room (*bathroom*, *kitchen*).

An EXCLAMATION or SILLY WORD is any sort of funny sound, gasp, grunt, or outcry, like *Wow!*, *Ouch!*, *Whomp!*, *Ick!*, and *Gadzooks!*

When we ask for specific words, like a NUMBER, a COLOR, an ANIMAL, or a PART OF THE BODY, we mean a word that is one of those things, like *seven*, *blue*, *horse*, or *head*.

When we ask for a PLURAL, it means more than one. For example, *cat* pluralized is *cats*.

MAD LIBS® is fun to play with friends, but you can also play it by yourself! To begin with, DO NOT look at the story on the page below. Fill in the blanks on this page with the words called for. Then, using the words you have selected, fill in the blank spaces in the story.

Now you've created your own hilarious MAD LIBS® game!

## SOPHIE AND THE BFG

ADJECTIVE _____

NOUN _____

NOUN _____

ADJECTIVE _____

ADJECTIVE _____

NOUN _____

ADJECTIVE _____

ADJECTIVE _____

ADVERB _____

PLURAL NOUN _____

ADJECTIVE _____

NOUN _____

PLURAL NOUN _____

ADJECTIVE _____

# THE BFG

# MAD LIBS®

# SOPHIE AND THE BFG

One _____ night, a little orphan _____ named
          ADJECTIVE                                    NOUN

Sophie couldn't sleep. It was the witching hour—a special moment in

the middle of the night when every child and every _____ is
                                                        NOUN

in a deep, deep sleep, and all the _____ things come out
                                        ADJECTIVE

from hiding. Sophie peeked out from the curtains and saw a/an

_____ sight—a giant person wearing a long black
   ADJECTIVE

_____, carrying a long, thin trumpet and a/an _____
   NOUN                                                      ADJECTIVE

suitcase. When he spied Sophie, he picked her up and whisked her

away to a/an _____ cave in Giant Country. "Ha! What has us
                ADJECTIVE

got here?" asked the Giant. "Please don't eat me!" said Sophie. The

Giant laughed _____. "Me gobbling up human
                    ADVERB

_____? This I never," he said. "I is the Big _____
   PLURAL NOUN                                              ADJECTIVE

Giant. I is the BFG. What is *your* name?" "My _____ is
                                                    NOUN

Sophie," Sophie said. And that is how these two _____
                                                     PLURAL NOUN

became _____ friends.
            ADJECTIVE

MAD LIBS® is fun to play with friends, but you can also play it by yourself! To begin with, DO NOT look at the story on the page below. Fill in the blanks on this page with the words called for. Then, using the words you have selected, fill in the blank spaces in the story.

Now you've created your own hilarious MAD LIBS® game!

# THE BIG
# FRIENDLY _____
NOUN

PLURAL NOUN _____

ADJECTIVE _____

NOUN _____

NOUN _____

ADJECTIVE _____

PLURAL NOUN _____

NUMBER _____

ADJECTIVE _____

VERB ENDING IN "ING" _____

VERB ENDING IN "ING" _____

ADJECTIVE _____

PLURAL NOUN _____

NOUN _____

PLURAL NOUN _____

# THE BFG

## MAD LIBS®
## THE BIG
## FRIENDLY _____
####### NOUN

I is the Big Friendly Giant. I live in Giant Country, but I is not like the

other _____. Most giants is all cannybully and likes to
###### PLURAL NOUN

gobble up human beans, but I is much too _____ and jumbly.
############## ADJECTIVE

Instead, I eat an icky-poo _____ called the snozzcumber. It is
################## NOUN

filthing, but it is the only _____ that grows in Giant Country.
######################### NOUN

For a giant, I is a/an _____ runt. I is only twenty-four
##################### ADJECTIVE

_____ tall, and all of those maneating giants is at least
### PLURAL NOUN

_____ times my wideness and double my _____
## NUMBER                                         ADJECTIVE

highness. At night, when all the other giants is _____
########################## VERB ENDING IN "ING"

off every what way and which to swollop human beans, I is

_____ away to other places to blow lovely,
## VERB ENDING IN "ING"

_____ dreams into the bedrooms of sleeping _____.
## ADJECTIVE                                              PLURAL NOUN

I may be an unusual _____, and I may say things a little
#################### NOUN

squiggly, but I is much more pleasant than those human-bean-eating

_____!
## PLURAL NOUN

MAD LIBS® is fun to play with friends, but you can also play it by yourself! To begin with, DO NOT look at the story on the page below. Fill in the blanks on this page with the words called for. Then, using the words you have selected, fill in the blank spaces in the story.

Now you've created your own hilarious MAD LIBS® game!

# GIANT COUNTRY

ADJECTIVE _____

ADJECTIVE _____

COLOR _____

ADJECTIVE _____

ADVERB _____

PLURAL NOUN _____

ADJECTIVE _____

VERB ENDING IN "ING" _____

ADJECTIVE _____

PLURAL NOUN _____

ADJECTIVE _____

NOUN _____

# THE BFG

# MAD LIBS

# GIANT COUNTRY

Far, far away, across oceans and distant lands, is a/an _____
                                                          ADJECTIVE

wasteland. The ground is _____ and pale yellow, with great
                              ADJECTIVE

lumps of _____ rock scattered around. _____ trees
              COLOR                                        ADJECTIVE

stand everywhere like skeletons. The sun beats down _____
                                                          ADVERB

on this dry, barren place—deserted except for the huge

_____ that live there. This is _____ Giant
   PLURAL NOUN                                 ADJECTIVE

Country. Here, the giants spend their days _____ and
                                              VERB ENDING IN "ING"

lounging on _____ rocks, waiting for the night to come, when
                ADJECTIVE

they will travel all over the world in search of tasty _____
                                                          PLURAL NOUN

to eat. And in a cave inside a/an _____ mountain, there dwells
                                      ADJECTIVE

the Big Friendly _____.
                      NOUN

MAD LIBS® is fun to play with friends, but you can also play it by yourself! To begin with, DO NOT look at the story on the page below. Fill in the blanks on this page with the words called for. Then, using the words you have selected, fill in the blank spaces in the story.

Now you've created your own hilarious MAD LIBS® game!

# THE GIANTS

NOUN _____

TYPE OF LIQUID _____

NOUN _____

NOUN _____

NOUN _____

NOUN _____

NOUN _____

NOUN _____

NOUN _____

PART OF THE BODY (PLURAL) _____

COLOR _____

PART OF THE BODY (PLURAL) _____

PART OF THE BODY (PLURAL) _____

PART OF THE BODY _____

ADJECTIVE _____

NOUN _____

PART OF THE BODY _____

NOUN _____

# THE BFG

# MAD LIBS®

# THE GIANTS

The human-bean-eating giants are a/an _____ to behold.
                                          NOUN

They are named Fleshlumpeater, _____-bottler,
                                      TYPE OF LIQUID

_____-hugger, _____-cruncher, _____-chewer,
      NOUN                    NOUN                      NOUN

_____-dripper, _____-gulper, _____-masher,
      NOUN                    NOUN                    NOUN

and Butcher _____. They are completely naked, except for
                  NOUN

short skirts around their _____. Their skins are
                          PART OF THE BODY (PLURAL)

_____ from all the time spent in the sun. They have
        COLOR

huge bellies, long arms, and big _____. Their faces
                                 PART OF THE BODY (PLURAL)

are round and squished-looking, with small, flat _____.
                                                 PART OF THE BODY (PLURAL)

But their mouths are huge, spreading from ear to _____.
                                                  PART OF THE BODY

Their lips are like _____ sausages lying on top of one
                         ADJECTIVE

another. Their tongues are jet-black, like big slabs of raw _____.
                                                                 NOUN

They even have hair growing out of their _____. The giants
                                          PART OF THE BODY

are uglier than a/an _____, and their breath is worse!
                          NOUN

MAD LIBS® is fun to play with friends, but you can also play it by yourself! To begin with, DO NOT look at the story on the page below. Fill in the blanks on this page with the words called for. Then, using the words you have selected, fill in the blank spaces in the story.

Now you've created your own hilarious MAD LIBS® game!

# THE BFG'S
# MARVELLOUS EARS

NOUN _____

NOUN _____

VERB ENDING IN "ING" _____

NOUN _____

PLURAL NOUN _____

PART OF THE BODY (PLURAL) _____

PLURAL NOUN _____

NOUN _____

NOUN _____

VERB _____

NOUN _____

PART OF THE BODY (PLURAL) _____

# THE BFG

# MAD LIBS®
## THE BFG'S
## MARVELLOUS EARS

The BFG has the biggest pair of ears you've ever seen in your entire

_____. And they can hear every little _____, too.
        NOUN                                        NOUN

The BFG can hear a ladybug _____ on a leaf. He can
                              VERB ENDING IN "ING"

hear the heartbeat of a small _____. He can hear
                                      NOUN

_____ talking to one another, although he can't understand
   PLURAL NOUN

what they're saying. And, on a clear night, if he swivels his

_____ this way and that, he can hear faraway music
PART OF THE BODY (PLURAL)

from the _____ in the sky. Did you know that plants and
           PLURAL NOUN

trees make noises, too? When the BFG picks a beautiful _____
                                                              NOUN

from a garden, he can hear it screaming as he twists its _____!
                                                                NOUN

But the most interesting thing of all is that the BFG can hear dreams

as they buzz and _____ through the air—and then he catches
                        VERB

them in a/an _____ to pour into the _____
                   NOUN                        PART OF THE BODY (PLURAL)

of sleeping children.

MAD LIBS® is fun to play with friends, but you can also play it by yourself! To begin with, DO NOT look at the story on the page below. Fill in the blanks on this page with the words called for. Then, using the words you have selected, fill in the blank spaces in the story.

Now you've created your own hilarious MAD LIBS® game!

# SNOZZCUMBERS

NOUN _____

ADJECTIVE _____

ADJECTIVE _____

ADVERB _____

ADJECTIVE _____

NOUN _____

COLOR _____

COLOR _____

PLURAL NOUN _____

PART OF THE BODY _____

NOUN _____

PLURAL NOUN _____

ADJECTIVE _____

PLURAL NOUN _____

A PLACE _____

NOUN _____

# THE BFG

# MAD LIBS®

# SNOZZCUMBERS

Nothing grows in Giant Country. Nothing except for one icky-poo

_____—the snozzcumber. Since the BFG doesn't eat people
   NOUN

like the other _____ giants, he has no choice but to live
       ADJECTIVE

entirely on a diet of _____ snozzcumbers. What is a
         ADJECTIVE

snozzcumber, you ask _____! It is a vegetable as big as a/an
       ADVERB

_____ man, and as thick as a/an _____. It is
 ADJECTIVE                           NOUN

_____ with _____ stripes along its length, and it's
  COLOR           COLOR

covered all over with coarse _____. The taste, though, is
               PLURAL NOUN

the most disgusting thing your _____ can imagine. It tastes
            PART OF THE BODY

like _____-skins and rotten _____. It tastes like
   NOUN               PLURAL NOUN

_____ cockroaches and slime-_____. It is so
 ADJECTIVE                 PLURAL NOUN

horrible, it is all the BFG can do not to spit it all over (the)

_____. Alas, the poor BFG has no choice but to eat this icky-
 A PLACE

poo _____ for every meal!
   NOUN

MAD LIBS® is fun to play with friends, but you can also play it by yourself! To begin with, DO NOT look at the story on the page below. Fill in the blanks on this page with the words called for. Then, using the words you have selected, fill in the blank spaces in the story.

Now you've created your own hilarious MAD LIBS® game!

# FROBSCOTTLE AND WHIZZPOPPERS

ADJECTIVE _____

COLOR _____

NOUN _____

TYPE OF LIQUID _____

NOUN _____

ADJECTIVE _____

PART OF THE BODY _____

PART OF THE BODY _____

NOUN _____

A PLACE _____

NOUN _____

PART OF THE BODY (PLURAL) _____

VERB _____

PART OF THE BODY _____

# THE BFG

# MAD LIBS®
## FROBSCOTTLE
## AND WHIZZPOPPERS

Frobscottle is a/an _____ beverage that giants like to drink. It
                     ADJECTIVE

is _____ and fizzy, and it is as sweet and tasty as a/an
     COLOR

_____. It tastes of vanilla and _____, with a
  NOUN                                    TYPE OF LIQUID

trace of _____-berries. But the bubbles in frobscottle go down
          NOUN

instead of up! When people drink soda, with the bubbles going up,

they might let a/an _____ burp out of their _____.
                    ADJECTIVE                        PART OF THE BODY

When giants drink frobscottle, however, the bubbles come out of

their _____! Giants call this a whizzpopper. While humans
      PART OF THE BODY

consider whizzpoppers to be very rude, especially in a public

_____ like (the) _____, giants consider whizzpoppers
  NOUN                    A PLACE

to be a sign of a happy _____. They whizzpop all the time! It
                         NOUN

is music to their _____. Best of all, when giants
                  PART OF THE BODY (PLURAL)

whizzpop, they lift off of the ground and briefly _____ in the
                                                   VERB

air. So drink some frobscottle and whizzpop to your _____'s
                                                    PART OF THE BODY

content!

MAD LIBS® is fun to play with friends, but you can also play it by yourself! To begin with, DO NOT look at the story on the page below. Fill in the blanks on this page with the words called for. Then, using the words you have selected, fill in the blank spaces in the story.

Now you've created your own hilarious MAD LIBS® game!

# HOW TO SPEAK LIKE THE BFG

ADJECTIVE _____

VERB _____

PLURAL NOUN _____

PART OF THE BODY (PLURAL) _____

SAME PART OF THE BODY (PLURAL) _____

ADJECTIVE _____

ANIMAL (PLURAL) _____

ADJECTIVE _____

# THE BFG

# MAD LIBS
# HOW TO SPEAK
# LIKE THE BFG

"Words is oh such a twitch-tickling problem to me all my life," says the

BFG. And he certainly comes up with a lot of _____ words
                                            ADJECTIVE

and phrases! If you'd like to _____ like the BFG, here's a list
                              VERB

of some of his most delightful _____:
                               PLURAL NOUN

- **Human beans** are what the BFG calls people. He does

  *not* mean they are vegetables. As he says, "The human bean

  has two _____ and a vegetable has no
          PART OF THE BODY (PLURAL)

  _____ at all."
  SAME PART OF THE BODY (PLURAL)

- **Hippodumplings**, **crocadowndillies**, **cattlepiddlers**, and

  **elefunts** are just a few of the _____ names the BFG
                                      ADJECTIVE

  has come up with for animals. Hippodumplings are hippos,

  crocadowndillies are crocodiles, cattlepiddlers are caterpillars,

  and elefunts are, of course, _____.
                               ANIMAL (PLURAL)

- **Icky-poo** and **ucky-mucky** are a couple of words the BFG

  likes to use to describe gross things, like the _____
                                                  ADJECTIVE

  snozzcumber.

MAD LIBS® is fun to play with friends, but you can also play it by yourself! To begin with, DO NOT look at the story on the page below. Fill in the blanks on this page with the words called for. Then, using the words you have selected, fill in the blank spaces in the story.

Now you've created your own hilarious MAD LIBS® game!

# HOW TO SPEAK LIKE THE BFG, CONTINUED

PLURAL NOUN _____

PLURAL NOUN _____

PERSON IN ROOM _____

ADJECTIVE _____

PART OF THE BODY (PLURAL) _____

NOUN _____

ADVERB _____

VERB _____

PART OF THE BODY _____

PART OF THE BODY _____

- **Rotrasper** and **fizzwiggler** are what the BFG calls mean and

  nasty _____, like the _____ at Sophie's
  <u>PLURAL NOUN</u>                 <u>PLURAL NOUN</u>

  orphanage or _____.
               <u>PERSON IN ROOM</u>

- If you are **swizzfiggling** or **fibbling**, you are telling a/an

  _____ tale. In other words, you're lying through your
  <u>ADJECTIVE</u>

  _____.
  <u>PART OF THE BODY (PLURAL)</u>

- If the BFG doesn't like a/an _____, he **squoggles**,
                                <u>NOUN</u>

  **mispises**, or **dispunges** it. In other words, he _____
                                                        <u>ADVERB</u>

  dislikes it.

- If something is so disgusting, it makes your stomach

  _____, the BFG says it is **disgusterous**, **sickable**,
  <u>VERB</u>

  **rotsome**, or **maggotwise**.

- On the other _____, if something is delightful, the
               <u>PART OF THE BODY</u>

  BFG calls it **wondercrump**, **whoopsy-splunkers**, or **squiffling**.

- When the BFG puts something delicious in his _____,
                                               <u>PART OF THE BODY</u>

  like frobscottle for example, he calls it **glummy**. Yum!

MAD LIBS® is fun to play with friends, but you can also play it by yourself! To begin with, DO NOT look at the story on the page below. Fill in the blanks on this page with the words called for. Then, using the words you have selected, fill in the blank spaces in the story.

Now you've created your own hilarious MAD LIBS® game!

# CATCHING DREAMS IN DREAM COUNTRY

ADJECTIVE _____

ADJECTIVE _____

PART OF THE BODY _____

VERB _____

PLURAL NOUN _____

PART OF THE BODY (PLURAL) _____

VERB (PAST TENSE) _____

NOUN _____

NOUN _____

PLURAL NOUN _____

ADJECTIVE _____

NOUN _____

A PLACE _____

The BFG took Sophie all the way to a/an _____ place where

__ADJECTIVE__

the land is flat and _____, and mist swirls around as far as the

__ADJECTIVE__

_____ can see. "We is in Dream Country," the BFG said.

__PART OF THE BODY__

"This is where all dreams _____." The BFG opened his

__VERB__

suitcase and took out several glass _____. The BFG's

__PLURAL NOUN__

_____ swiveled this way and that until, suddenly, he

__PART OF THE BODY (PLURAL)__

_____ into the air and swung his net through the

__VERB (PAST TENSE)__

mist. "Got him!" he cried. Sophie handed him a/an _____

__NOUN__

and the BFG put the dream inside and closed the lid. The BFG

inspected the dream, exclaiming, "It's a phizzwizard!" A phizzwizard,

he explained, is a very happy dream, sure to make a/an _____

__NOUN__

dream of magic and ponies and _____. But when the next

__PLURAL NOUN__

dream was a/an _____ nightmare, the BFG was done.

__ADJECTIVE__

"_____-catching is finished for today," he announced. And

__NOUN__

he packed his suitcase, whisking Sophie back to (the) _____.

__A PLACE__

MAD LIBS® is fun to play with friends, but you can also play it by yourself! To begin with, DO NOT look at the story on the page below. Fill in the blanks on this page with the words called for. Then, using the words you have selected, fill in the blank spaces in the story.

Now you've created your own hilarious MAD LIBS® game!

# A TROGGLEHUMPER

ADJECTIVE _____

PLURAL NOUN _____

ADJECTIVE _____

NOUN _____

PART OF THE BODY (PLURAL) _____

NOUN _____

ADVERB _____

NOUN _____

ADJECTIVE _____

NOUN _____

A PLACE _____

PERSON IN ROOM _____

PERSON IN ROOM _____

CELEBRITY _____

PART OF THE BODY _____

# THE BFG

## MAD LIBS

# A TROGGLEHUMPER

A trogglehumper is what the BFG calls a/an _____ nightmare.
<u>ADJECTIVE</u>

Here are some of the most common nightmares experienced by

_____ like you and me:
<u>PLURAL NOUN</u>

- Being chased by a/an _____ _____, but your
  <u>ADJECTIVE</u>  <u>NOUN</u>

  _____ won't move fast enough.
  <u>PART OF THE BODY (PLURAL)</u>

- Forgetting to study for a test in _____ class and failing
  <u>NOUN</u>

  _____.
  <u>ADVERB</u>

- Falling off of a very tall _____.
  <u>NOUN</u>

- Being caught in the middle of a/an _____ disaster such
  <u>ADJECTIVE</u>

  as a flood, tornado, or _____-storm.
  <u>NOUN</u>

- Getting lost in (the) _____.
  <u>A PLACE</u>

- Giving a speech in front of everyone you know, including

  _____, _____, and _____, and
  <u>PERSON IN ROOM</u>  <u>PERSON IN ROOM</u>  <u>CELEBRITY</u>

  realizing you're wearing no clothes on your _____!
  <u>PART OF THE BODY</u>

MAD LIBS® is fun to play with friends, but you can also play it by yourself! To begin with, DO NOT look at the story on the page below. Fill in the blanks on this page with the words called for. Then, using the words you have selected, fill in the blank spaces in the story.

Now you've created your own hilarious MAD LIBS® game!

# HOW TO MIX A
# DREAM, BY THE BFG

PLURAL NOUN _____

PLURAL NOUN _____

ADJECTIVE _____

ADJECTIVE _____

ADJECTIVE _____

VERB ENDING IN "ING" _____

NOUN _____

ADJECTIVE _____

VERB ENDING IN "ING _____

NOUN _____

ADJECTIVE _____

ADVERB _____

NOUN _____

ADJECTIVE _____

PLURAL NOUN _____

ADJECTIVE _____

# MAD LIBS®
# HOW TO MIX A
# DREAM, BY THE BFG

Mixing a dream is a bit like mixing flour, sugar, and _____
                                                       PLURAL NOUN

to make a cake. If you is putting the right _____ into it,
                                              PLURAL NOUN

you is making the cake come out any way you want—sugary,

_____, Christmassy, or _____. It is the same with
   ADJECTIVE                          ADJECTIVE

_____ dreams. I has lots of dreams. I has dreams about
   ADJECTIVE

_____, dreams about a/an _____, and
VERB ENDING IN "ING"                              NOUN

dreams about having _____ wings. If you want a dream about
                          ADJECTIVE

_____ into a/an _____ with
VERB ENDING IN "ING"                    NOUN

_____ wings, you just pour all those dreams in a big jar and
   ADJECTIVE

stir _____ with a/an _____-beater. All the little
       ADVERB                         NOUN

_____ dream-bits that you don't need will turn into
   ADJECTIVE

_____ and float away. And you're left with just the
   PLURAL NOUN

_____ dream you want!
   ADJECTIVE

MAD LIBS® is fun to play with friends, but you can also play it by yourself! To begin with, DO NOT look at the story on the page below. Fill in the blanks on this page with the words called for. Then, using the words you have selected, fill in the blank spaces in the story.

Now you've created your own hilarious MAD LIBS® game!

# DREAM JAR #4,462

ADJECTIVE _____

NOUN _____

ADJECTIVE _____

LAST NAME _____

PART OF THE BODY _____

NOUN _____

ADJECTIVE _____

A PLACE _____

NOUN _____

ADJECTIVE _____

NOUN _____

LAST NAME _____

PART OF THE BODY (PLURAL) _____

NOUN _____

# MAD LIBS

# DREAM JAR #4,462

On each of his dream jars, the BFG writes a/an _____
                                                ADJECTIVE
description. Here is one of them:

The _____ rings in our house and my father picks it up and
        NOUN

says in his very _____ tellyphone voice, "_____
                    ADJECTIVE                         LAST NAME

speaking." Then his _____ goes white and he says,
                      PART OF THE BODY

"What! Who? Yes, sir, I understand, sir, but surely it is me you is

wishing to speak to, sir, not my little _____?" And he turns to
                                          NOUN

me and he says in a rather _____ voice, "Is you knowing the
                              ADJECTIVE

president of (the) _____?" and I says, "No, but I expect he has
                      A PLACE

heard all about my _____." Then I is having a/an
                      NOUN

_____ talk on the phone and saying things like, "Let me take
  ADJECTIVE

care of your _____, President _____," and my
                NOUN                      LAST NAME

father's _____ are popping right out of his
          PART OF THE BODY (PLURAL)

_____!
    NOUN

MAD LIBS® is fun to play with friends, but you can also play it by yourself! To begin with, DO NOT look at the story on the page below. Fill in the blanks on this page with the words called for. Then, using the words you have selected, fill in the blank spaces in the story.

Now you've created your own hilarious MAD LIBS® game!

# DREAM JAR #56

ADJECTIVE _____

PART OF THE BODY _____

ADJECTIVE _____

PART OF THE BODY (PLURAL) _____

PART OF THE BODY (PLURAL) _____

NOUN _____

PERSON IN ROOM (MALE) _____

NOUN _____

VERB ENDING IN "ING" _____

ADVERB _____

VERB ENDING IN "ING" _____

PART OF THE BODY _____

# THE BFG

## MAD LIBS®

## DREAM JAR #56

This is another _____ description of the contents of one of
                         ADJECTIVE

the BFG's dream jars:

I is having a bath and I is discovering that if I press quite hard on my

_____, a/an _____ feeling comes over me and
PART OF THE BODY          ADJECTIVE

suddenly my _____ is not there nor is my
              PART OF THE BODY (PLURAL)

_____. In fact, I has become invisible and you can
PART OF THE BODY (PLURAL)

see right through my _____! So my mummy comes in and
                           NOUN

says, "Where is _____! He was in the bath a minute ago
                  PERSON IN ROOM (MALE)

and he can't possibly wash his _____ properly!" So I says, "Here I
                                    NOUN

is, _____ in the bathtub!" My mummy yells to my
     VERB ENDING IN "ING"

daddy to come _____. And my daddy says, "The soap is
                     ADVERB

_____ in the air all by itself!" Then I press my
VERB ENDING IN "ING"

_____ again, and now I is visible.
PART OF THE BODY

MAD LIBS® is fun to play with friends, but you can also play it by yourself! To begin with, DO NOT look at the story on the page below. Fill in the blanks on this page with the words called for. Then, using the words you have selected, fill in the blank spaces in the story.

Now you've created your own hilarious MAD LIBS® game!

# DREAM JAR #85,324,234

ADJECTIVE _____

ADJECTIVE _____

SAME ADJECTIVE _____

NOUN _____

VERB ENDING IN "ING" _____

A PLACE _____

VERB ENDING IN "ING" _____

PLURAL NOUN _____

PART OF THE BODY (PLURAL) _____

PART OF THE BODY (PLURAL) _____

PLURAL NOUN _____

A PLACE _____

PART OF THE BODY (PLURAL) _____

VERB ENDING IN "ING" _____

ADJECTIVE _____

A PLACE _____

# THE BFG

# MAD LIBS®

# DREAM JAR #85,324,234

Here's one more of the BFG's _____ dream descriptions:
ADJECTIVE

I has written a/an _____ book, and it is so _____,
ADJECTIVE  SAME ADJECTIVE

no one can put it down. As soon as you has read the first _____,
NOUN

you is so hooked on it you cannot stop _____ until
VERB ENDING IN "ING"

the last page. In (the) _____, people is _____
A PLACE  VERB ENDING IN "ING"

in the streets, bumping into _____ because their
PLURAL NOUN

_____ is buried in my book. Dentists is reading it
PART OF THE BODY (PLURAL)

when they is supposed to be fixing people's _____,
PART OF THE BODY (PLURAL)

but nobody minds because they is all reading it, too. Drivers is

reading it while driving their _____, and they is crashing
PLURAL NOUN

them all over (the) _____. Surgeons is reading it while they is
A PLACE

operating on _____. When I wake up I is
PART OF THE BODY (PLURAL)

still _____ with excitement at being the most
VERB ENDING IN "ING"

_____ writer in (the) _____.
ADJECTIVE  A PLACE

MAD LIBS® is fun to play with friends, but you can also play it by yourself! To begin with, DO NOT look at the story on the page below. Fill in the blanks on this page with the words called for. Then, using the words you have selected, fill in the blank spaces in the story.

Now you've created your own hilarious MAD LIBS® game!

# THE GREAT PLAN

PLURAL NOUN _____

A PLACE _____

ADJECTIVE _____

A PLACE _____

PLURAL NOUN _____

ADJECTIVE _____

PLURAL NOUN _____

ADJECTIVE _____

PLURAL NOUN _____

PLURAL NOUN _____

NOUN _____

VERB ENDING IN "ING" _____

ADJECTIVE _____

ADJECTIVE _____

# THE BFG

## MAD LIBS®

## THE GREAT PLAN

When Sophie and the BFG discover that the giants' plan is to eat

schoolfuls of _____ in (the) _____, they come up
                 PLURAL NOUN                    A PLACE

with a/an _____ plan to stop them. They will go to the Queen
              ADJECTIVE

of (the) _____ and ask for her help! But, they realize the Queen
              A PLACE

would never believe Sophie—she'd think Sophie had lost her

_____. So they decide to make the Queen dream all about
   PLURAL NOUN

_____ giants eating _____ from schools all over
   ADJECTIVE                        PLURAL NOUN

the country. She will also dream that there is a big, _____ giant
                                                           ADJECTIVE

who can tell her where all the bad _____ live so that she can
                                         PLURAL NOUN

send her armies of _____ to capture them once and for all.
                        PLURAL NOUN

And she will dream that a little _____ called Sophie will help
                                       NOUN

her find the BFG. The Queen will wake up and discover Sophie

_____ on her window ledge. Sophie will tell the
VERB ENDING IN "ING"

Queen her dream was a/an _____ reality. And the Queen will
                              ADJECTIVE

have no choice but to stop the _____ giants!
                                    ADJECTIVE

MAD LIBS® is fun to play with friends, but you can also play it by yourself! To begin with, DO NOT look at the story on the page below. Fill in the blanks on this page with the words called for. Then, using the words you have selected, fill in the blank spaces in the story.

Now you've created your own hilarious MAD LIBS® game!

# A VISIT TO THE QUEEN OF ENGLAND

ADVERB _____

PART OF THE BODY _____

ADJECTIVE _____

PLURAL NOUN _____

ADJECTIVE _____

A PLACE _____

LAST NAME _____

VERB (PAST TENSE) _____

PERSON IN ROOM (FEMALE) _____

ADVERB _____

ADJECTIVE _____

ADVERB _____

NOUN _____

ADJECTIVE _____

VERB ENDING IN "ING" _____

NOUN _____

ADJECTIVE _____

ADJECTIVE _____

# THE BFG

# MAD LIBS®
# A VISIT TO THE
# QUEEN OF ENGLAND

Sophie traveled in style from Giant Country back to England, nestled

_____ in the BFG's soft _____. On the way, they
         ADVERB                              PART OF THE BODY

passed the giants returning from a/an _____ night of eating
                                              ADJECTIVE

small _____. After a long and _____ journey,
         PLURAL NOUN                              ADJECTIVE

they arrived to (the) _____ in the middle of the night. They
                          A PLACE

found _____ Palace, and the BFG _____
         LAST NAME                                VERB (PAST TENSE)

over the gates and into Queen _____'s backyard. The
                                 PERSON IN ROOM (FEMALE)

BFG found the Queen's bedroom, opened the window, and placed

Sophie _____ on the ledge. Then he blew the _____
            ADVERB                                          ADJECTIVE

dream into the room. Then, all they could do was wait _____
                                                              ADVERB

for the _____ to rise and for the Queen to wake from her
            NOUN

_____ slumber. When the Queen awoke to find Sophie
   ADJECTIVE

_____ on her windowsill, she turned white as a/an
   VERB ENDING IN "ING"

_____. She quickly learned that her _____ nightmare
   NOUN                                           ADJECTIVE

had been real—and that Sophie and the BFG were going to help her

stop the _____ giants.
            ADJECTIVE

MAD LIBS® is fun to play with friends, but you can also play it by yourself! To begin with, DO NOT look at the story on the page below. Fill in the blanks on this page with the words called for. Then, using the words you have selected, fill in the blank spaces in the story.

Now you've created your own hilarious MAD LIBS® game!

## THE ROYAL BREAKFAST

ADJECTIVE _____

ADJECTIVE _____

PLURAL NOUN _____

PERSON IN ROOM (MALE) _____

NOUN _____

NOUN _____

PLURAL NOUN _____

PLURAL NOUN _____

ADJECTIVE _____

NOUN _____

SILLY WORD _____

PLURAL NOUN _____

NOUN _____

LAST NAME _____

ADJECTIVE _____

PART OF THE BODY _____

NOUN _____

ADVERB _____

# THE BFG

# THE ROYAL BREAKFAST

Once the Queen got over her _____ shock, she politely
                                ADJECTIVE

invited Sophie and the BFG for a/an _____ breakfast in the
                                       ADJECTIVE

ballroom. The Queen's servants built a table for the BFG using four

_____ and Prince _____'s ping-pong table.
   PLURAL NOUN                  PERSON IN ROOM (MALE)

They placed a/an _____ on top of a grand _____ for
                     NOUN                              NOUN

a chair. And they gathered gardening _____ and a sword
                                          PLURAL NOUN

for utensils. When it was time to eat, footmen carried in silver trays

of fried _____, bacon, sausages, and _____
            PLURAL NOUN                              ADJECTIVE

potatoes. The BFG had only ever eaten snozzcumbers and this food

made him happier than a/an _____. "By _____!" he
                               NOUN                SILLY WORD

hollered. "This stuff is making snozzcumbers taste like _____."
                                                          PLURAL NOUN

He ate so much, there was no _____ left at _____
                                 NOUN                LAST NAME

Palace. Then, the BFG let a/an _____ whizzpopper out of his
                                   ADJECTIVE

_____! Sophie could not believe the BFG had whizzpopped
PART OF THE BODY

in front of Her Majesty the _____, but luckily the Queen just
                                NOUN

laughed _____.
           ADVERB

MAD LIBS® is fun to play with friends, but you can also play it by yourself! To begin with, DO NOT look at the story on the page below. Fill in the blanks on this page with the words called for. Then, using the words you have selected, fill in the blank spaces in the story.

Now you've created your own hilarious MAD LIBS® game!

## GIANTS: CAUGHT!

A PLACE _____

NOUN _____

ADJECTIVE _____

ADJECTIVE _____

ADJECTIVE _____

NOUN _____

A PLACE _____

ADJECTIVE _____

PERSON IN ROOM (FEMALE) _____

ADJECTIVE _____

PART OF THE BODY (PLURAL) _____

ADJECTIVE _____

PERSON IN ROOM _____

PART OF THE BODY _____

NOUN _____

ADJECTIVE _____

A PLACE _____

ADJECTIVE _____

# THE BFG

# MAD LIBS®

# GIANTS: CAUGHT!

LONDON, (the) _____—Today, the Royal Air
⎯⎯⎯⎯⎯ A PLACE

_____ and the _____ Army engaged in a/an
NOUN           ADJECTIVE

_____ operation in the _____ place Giant Country,
ADJECTIVE          ADJECTIVE

recently discovered to be the home of nine _____-eating
NOUN

giants who have been terrorizing countries all over (the) _____.
A PLACE

Led by a good giant named the BFG and his companion, a/an

_____ girl named _____, a team of
ADJECTIVE         PERSON IN ROOM (FEMALE)

helicopters flew to Giant Country, tracked down the _____
ADJECTIVE

giants, and tied their arms and _____ together.
PART OF THE BODY (PLURAL)

Before they were finished, however, one _____ giant got hold
ADJECTIVE

of a brave soldier named _____. Thankfully the little girl
PERSON IN ROOM

poked the giant in the _____ with Her Royal Highness's
PART OF THE BODY

brooch, and the giant let go of the poor, frightened _____.
NOUN

The air force and army got on with their _____ business,
ADJECTIVE

airlifting all nine giants back to (the) _____. The soldiers, the
A PLACE

BFG, and the little girl were _____ heroes, one and all.
ADJECTIVE

MAD LIBS® is fun to play with friends, but you can also play it by yourself! To begin with, DO NOT look at the story on the page below. Fill in the blanks on this page with the words called for. Then, using the words you have selected, fill in the blank spaces in the story.

Now you've created your own hilarious MAD LIBS® game!

# DO NOT FEED THE GIANTS

ADJECTIVE _____

A PLACE _____

NOUN _____

ADJECTIVE _____

PERSON IN ROOM _____

PART OF THE BODY _____

PERSON IN ROOM _____

SAME PERSON IN ROOM _____

LAST NAME _____

NOUN _____

PART OF THE BODY (PLURAL) _____

A PLACE _____

A PLACE _____

PERSON IN ROOM _____

ADJECTIVE _____

A PLACE _____

ADVERB _____

ADJECTIVE _____

# DO NOT FEED THE GIANTS

One day, for a/an _____ class trip, some schoolchildren got
              ADJECTIVE

on a bus and traveled to (the) _____ to see the famous
                              A PLACE

_____-eating giants. "I can't wait to see those _____
NOUN                                                    ADJECTIVE

beasts!" said little _____. "I'm scared! What if one tries
                    PERSON IN ROOM

to eat my _____?" said _____. "It's okay,
          PART OF THE BODY          PERSON IN ROOM

_____, dear," said their teacher, Mrs.
SAME PERSON IN ROOM

_____. "The giants live in a hole twice the size of a/an
LAST NAME

_____-ball field. You'll be very safe!" When the school bus
NOUN

arrived, the children could not believe their _____.
                                            PART OF THE BODY (PLURAL)

Crowds had traveled from near and far—from places such as (the)

_____ and (the) _____—just to see the giants.
A PLACE                  A PLACE

"Look!" said _____. "It's feeding time!" "Ah, yes," said their
            PERSON IN ROOM

teacher. "The giants are being forced to eat _____
                                            ADJECTIVE

snozzcumbers. They are the most disgusting vegetable in all of (the)

_____!" The children laughed _____. Those
A PLACE                                ADVERB

_____ giants were getting exactly what they deserved!
ADJECTIVE

MAD LIBS® is fun to play with friends, but you can also play it by yourself! To begin with, DO NOT look at the story on the page below. Fill in the blanks on this page with the words called for. Then, using the words you have selected, fill in the blank spaces in the story.

Now you've created your own hilarious MAD LIBS® game!

## HAPPILY EVER AFTER

PLURAL NOUN _____

NOUN _____

PLURAL NOUN _____

PLURAL NOUN _____

A PLACE _____

LAST NAME _____

VERB _____

ADJECTIVE _____

NOUN _____

ADJECTIVE _____

PLURAL NOUN _____

PLURAL NOUN _____

NOUN _____

ADVERB _____

After Sophie and the BFG rescued the world from human-bean-eating

_____, they were handsomely rewarded for their
PLURAL NOUN

efforts. The _____ of India sent an elephant to the BFG. They
NOUN

received camels, _____, hats, and _____ from all
PLURAL NOUN                          PLURAL NOUN

over the world. But best of all, the Queen of (the) _____ gave
A PLACE

them each a home near _____ Castle. She had a gigantic house
LAST NAME

built for the BFG to _____ in, and next door was
VERB

a/an _____ cottage for Sophie. The BFG was given the title of
ADJECTIVE

the Royal Dream-_____, and he had a special room to store all
NOUN

the _____ dreams he collected. Sophie taught the BFG to read
ADJECTIVE

_____ and to write about _____. One day, the
PLURAL NOUN                          PLURAL NOUN

BFG became so good at writing, he wrote his own book about his

adventure with his dear _____ Sophie. And the BFG and
NOUN

Sophie lived _____ ever after.
ADVERB

**Download Mad Libs today!**

Join the millions of Mad Libs fans creating wacky and wonderful stories on our apps!